TOO MUCH AND NOT ENOUGH

LOUD HEARTS AND SILENT WARS

A poetry collection

by

Rachel Merryn

Published by Purple Storm Publishing, 2025

This is a work of poetry. Names, characters, businesses, places, events, and incidents are either the products of the author's imagination or used in a fictitious manner. Certain names and identifying details may have been changed to protect the privacy of individuals

TOO MUCH AND NOT ENOUGH: Loud Hearts and Silent Wars

First edition., December 25, 2025.

Written by Rachel Merryn.

Editor:
Emily Reed

Illustrators:
Rosie Boughen
Cecily at Punkbuggy Studio
Regar Adi at Fiverr
Sierra Jackson
Helaina Sears
Gigi Kona
Rachel Merryn

DEDICATION

For the self who carried these stories
and the self who dared to release them.
To the ice that burns and the flame that freezes in me:
You've both found your home here.

PREFACE

These pieces were written over the course of the last five years, yet they found their way into this collection within five months. Drawn from my own songs, unfinished poems, scattered ramblings, restless thoughts, and newly born ideas, they were gathered and refined into the form you now hold.

Each illustration throughout follows the poem that inspired it. I cannot thank enough the artists I get to call my friends who brought my prompts and ideas to life.

SECTION ONE:
BLACK UMBRELLAS
&
WHITE LILIES

Grief has no rules.

12/25

Today marks a year without you here
The same flowers from that day
Sit on our kitchen windowsill
Like it or not, life without you moves still.

I hear your voice
In the background of all your favorite songs
I listen to them more now than when I was young
I wonder how we would've gotten along
As time went on
Had your illness not taken you from us for so long.

I've learned how to drink my coffee just like you
It does taste better the longer that it sits
Even more so with a sprinkle of cookie bits.

Six months after you, I finally made it to the ocean
It was everything you always said that it would be
When I looked out on that horizon
I wished you could be right there next to me.

The ghost of you is everywhere
It follows me endlessly
It's not supernatural
But it's super natural to miss you.

It's kinda funny how I find pieces of you all around me
Little reminders of how close one day we will be
Most days, I don't pay attention to
All the habits, phrases, and choices I have made
Because of you.

I can't bring myself to pitch
Those flowers in our kitchen
They've lasted this long
Getting rid of them would just feel wrong.

Today marks a year that we don't have you here
But it feels as though just yesterday we had you near
Yet as soon as tomorrow
This year could be a distant memory
I know once again you'll be with me.

Μανάρι

Όταν ήμουν πιο νεαρή, ζητούσα να φύγω μόνη
Νόμιζα η ζωή με περιμένει στην επόμενη πόλη
Μετρούσα μέρες, χρόνια, για να ανοίξει ο δρόμος
Να πω «μεγάλωσα», χωρίς κανέναν φόβο.

Κι όμως, πατέρα μου, τώρα που πέρασε ο χρόνος
Βλέπω πως έτρεχα μακριά απ' ό,τι ήταν δικό μου
Και όσο κι αν στάθηκα στα πόδια που ζητούσα
Γύρισα μέσα μου σε σένα που αγαπούσα.

Κι όταν έφυγες, πατέρα μου, η φωνή χάθηκε
Και η μουσική που αγαπούσα πια μαράθηκε
Θέλω να γυρίσω πίσω, να κρατήσω το παιδί
Το μανάρι σου που χόρευε και γελούσε απ' την ψυχή.

Funeral for Two

We gather here today
To mourn the now deceased
And the person I became for them
Both lives now released.

No flowers could dress it up
No sermon could console
We permanently bury here
Half a life, half a soul.

I know I'll meet you again
But never the "me" you once knew
That girl has also passed, laid down to rest
Her heartbeat followed you.

So many faces I've yet to meet
And none will know her name
She lives inside a memory
Untouched, eternally the same.

I can't decide if this is loss
Or mercy in disguise
To love and die within one life
Nothing left to reconcile.

Both lives well lived
Only one kept out of view
Both fading like morning fog
At this funeral for two.

The Stranger

I'm quick to snap
Raise my voice
And it's not just in play
There's something heavy underneath
I don't know how to say.

Windows reflect familiarity
Yet I'm startled every time I see
I've never met this version
My grief forced me to be.

I fight so viciously, the world believes
They see behind my every tear
How can they when even I don't recognize
The restlessness that rages here?

It feels like simple anger
Not like sadness in disguise
Underneath, a hollowed hurt
Is threatening to rise.

I walk around an open book
Available for all to see
Yet hidden from my former self
I remain a mystery.

I used to know my laughter's tone
The sound and sight of my own name
But sadness came and wore my face
And left it not the same.

I've met my gaze in glassy walls
I've felt that stranger stare
Waiting for something, watching
Unsure of who stands there.

Where there is loss, there is an open space
I guess I'm meeting someone new
A darker shade of what I was
But still a piece of true.

Pity the Living

If only the living were pitied
The way we mourn the dead
Not scrubbed of their sins
Left with only good to remember
Only once their last breath has been shed.

Why do we bury the harshness of memory?
Polish what's left?
What feels like pity
Is often not truly so, but rather
Guilt in a borrowed dress.

For we can't erase
What we hated when they still had breath
So we sanctify whatever goodness we can find
And magnify it
To soften the sting of death.

We tell ourselves stories
To smother the dirt and decay
Overlook any sign of ugly
Because we don't want to be the
Reason their legacy is forever frayed.

The living can be redeemed
They can stumble and mend
Pity arrives when all chances are gone
We like to call it "respect for the dead"
But I think the living deserve that pity instead.

Closure: the phantom
Recedes every time it is chased
A cruel little riddle
With no right answer
We're doomed to pursue in haste.

I hold onto bitterness as an armor
Refusing release
Because better that than
Trust a faulty memory
Influenced by a desire for peace.

We don't miss the person lost
So much as the possible futures they erase
"Maybes" become "nevers"
When they leave this awful place.

What we really miss are the chances
The doors that will never swing
It feels selfish, really
Hope buried with bodies
Still writhes like a living thing.

I can't fathom to admit it
But maybe my distance
My grief all along
Is just fear that I'd feel too little
Or maybe too strong.

The Weightless Truth

The truth weighs nothing
But it pulls like stone
It shouldn't hurt
Yet it cuts to the bone.

We all carry our weight differently
Some on our backs, determined and strong
Some in our gut, like a woman
Who knows when something is wrong.

Others hold their baggage in their minds
The excess spilling out in their words
Or in their legs, slowing them down
'Til they can barely move around.

Some carry it on their shoulders
Some in their hands
Shaping the way they move
Obeying silent commands.

I don't believe there exists many a human
Who are truly weightless and free
Who live without a care in the world
Like leaves in the breeze.

I don't believe that what we carry defines us
But merely explains
How we survived, why we breathe
What makes us feel alive.

TOO MUCH AND NOT ENOUGH

I think mine sits on my heart
Controlling my narrative
Of which my mind plays no part
It opens and closes, judges, perceives
Lays claim to whatever it wants
Regardless what I try to believe.

It teaches me kindness in all the wrong places
Softens my gaze for familiar faces
The ones who struggle like I used to
So I reach for them first
Though they never reach too.

It tells me who's safe
By how much they've been through
Drawn to those who know how to survive
I call it compassion, maybe it's pride
Loving to feel loved doesn't mean that love is a lie.

My face wears the load my heart can't disguise
A visible map of all the lows and highs
No mask can obscure what I'm feeling inside
The truth in my eyes is where I reside.

I think we're all just doing our best
With what's been handed down
Some carry sorrow like a secret
Some wear it like a crown.

There's no right way
To hold what hurts
Only ways to move through
I choose to believe the only weightless truth:
That what we carry reveals what is true.

The Body Remembers

I twist my hair when lost in thought
Not realizing how tightly I've pulled the knot
By the time ache blooms behind my eyes
I've braided worry in silent disguise.

You would think my feet would be sore
During long walks, it got easy to ignore
The pull of reflection easily outweighs
Any feelings of discomfort that come my way.

Biting nails never really made sense to me
Until I caught myself picking
Turns out a nervous tic isn't always a choice
It's often just how we turn down the noise.

The mind is a master of softening the blow
Rewriting chapters we think we know
Dimming edges, blurring our view
The body reacts before we do.

It's not just the brain that mourns what we lose
Our skin, our pulse, even taste will choose
To stand as witness to the past in ways we ignore
The body still knocking on memory's door.

After all this, we wonder and complain
"Why is my body always in pain?"
The body remembers what we do to the heart
Because healing and hurting are never too far apart.

Despair

Happiness exists, sure.
But it's just background noise
A cheap carnival prize
In life's long list of toys.

Despair throws a parade
Announces its grand arrival
While joy sneaks in slowly
Barely worth survival.

Why is joy reduced
To some average human norm
While misery cripples, barges in
Forms a perfect storm?

I chronically compare, you see
I can't help it, but I can
Because why enjoy in peace
When the world hands you lemons
And calls it a feast?

Laughter is reduced to a blip
Every sigh a headline in red
The brain keeps a ledger
Calculated storage
Of all the misery we've been fed.

TOO MUCH AND NOT ENOUGH

Delight is inevitably suspicious
Probably a trap
Sorrow? Her footsteps are memorized
She sits freely in my lap.

So yes, joy exists
Only in borrowed time
A punch line in a joke
That barely passes as rhyme.

Meanwhile despair rents
A penthouse in my head for free
And the irony? I call this "reality."

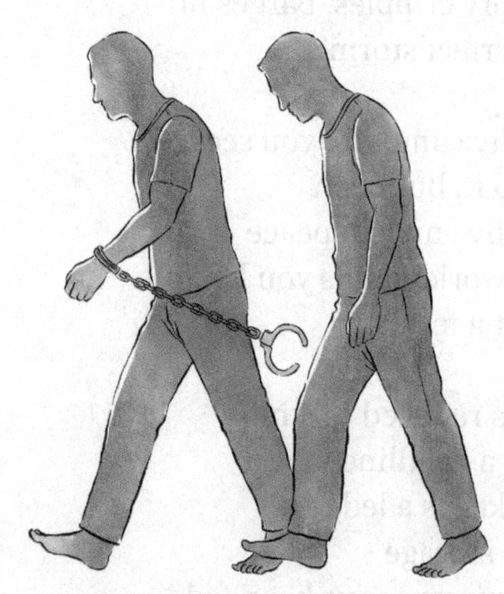

The Eyes

I don't know what to tell you
Why I crave attention
But freeze when you look me in the eyes
Please don't look me in the eyes.

Please acknowledge me silently
From a distance
And loudly in someone else's presence
I don't know what to tell you
I have no defenses.

Whether I laugh when it's serious
Because my body is trying, delirious
To regulate and calm my anxious self
Or because someone else
Used to do it, disruption in their brain
And I inherited it just the same.

My greatest fear is that
I picked up a lot more than a laugh
Along the crooked path to who I am.

I may never know which parts of you
Were yourself or illness bestowed
Pull bubble gum out of a hairbrush
To see which pieces of me are yours
And which are all my own.

TOO MUCH AND NOT ENOUGH

Your eyes stare back at mine
Every time I see my own
When will I stop wondering
What I may not ever know?

Dried Blood

Vitality that once was bright red
Is now a dried-up maroon
Its lacking, a healing to the skin
Endurance that ended too soon.

In the vortex of fragile sanity, I danced
A marionette twirling through the expanse
A frenzy let loose when danger is found
Too busy to ever sit down.

Bright blood meant I was alive
Each cut a sign I could fight
But stillness crept in when I did survive
And nothing now feels quite right.

Grief crusts on this old, closed wound
No longer fresh, but not gone
Vacancy that came too soon
A dusk mistaken for dawn.

Here I sit in the absence of flood
No surge, no rush, no sound
Just me and the weight of dried-up blood
Too numb to know I've drowned.

Reflections

Why does it always rain when we're sad?
How does the sky know I'm feeling so bad?

Obviously, it doesn't
It spills just the same
But when I'm breaking
It ripples my pain.

Raindrops are tears on heavy days
But also confetti that sparkles my gaze
Celestial drums can cry or shout loud and clear
The passion that moves me or the sob in my ear.

The world remains the same
But I shift and bend
Seeing myself
In the clouds that descend.

Sudden chills on a bright sunny day
Are calming whispers or doubt that won't go away
Fog wraps the earth like a tired sigh
Sometimes comfort, sometimes a guise.

I call the world beautiful when I feel the same
And cruel when I need something to blame
The earth reflects my mood like it knew
Not because it cares, but because I do.

Faulty Empathy

Your anguish is a deadweight
Anchored in my chest
I rush to fix the cracks in you
So I can find my rest.

At first, it's pure compassion
My only goal is to repair
But slowly, I just need you to be okay
So I can taste fresh air.

Your suffering becomes mine
Touching everything I do
I'm restless 'til you're smiling
'Til your world is bright and never blue.

It isn't selfless kindness
If my peace depends on yours
Empathy can tilt to greed
As it fights the battle to endure.

Those who seek to comfort
Often mask their own intent
Healing turns to hunger
For my own torments relent.

IYKYK

Sadness mirrored by music is catharsis at its finest
It hears me without the need for speech
Mimics my disposition without mockery
Cradles melancholy like a newborn emotion
Maturing it into description.

I Didn't Know Loss Could Grow Up Too

I remember crying over broken crayons
That felt like little bones
Losing a balloon to the sky
Was my first sense of alone.

When my mom was late to pick me up
It felt like she might never appear
When my dad left for the night shift
I ran after his car in fear.

Goodbyes that only lasted a weekend
Felt like forever in that small space
When someone else got the bigger slice
I felt the sting could never be erased.

Scraped knees and bedtime routines
Tragedies that ended by morning
When you're that little
Everything feels like the world is ending.

Because it is
At least the only one you've ever known
Children cry and scream
They're still learning
How much grief they can own.

The older we get
The small things stop hurting, sure
Our threshold grows, we endure.

Once you survive
You learn it was never deadly to begin
But when people leave
I still cry like a four-year-old again.

When Did This Happen?

I remember going to the movies as a kid
And bingeing all my favorite TV shows
Yelling at the screens
Impatient with every "too stupid to live" scene.

I'd never be moved all that much
And if I was, I'd immediately recede
Only ever interested to watch
If a happy ending was guaranteed.

Recently watching those same films
I can still recite every line
But I feel like I'm hearing
The story for the very first time.

Each act reflects a part of me
From the first frame to the last
I see variations of my own life
What if I did this? What if I did that?

Where once I saw just fiction
Now I see something more
The screen shows my own worn face
I didn't know before.

When did the switch inside me flip
And make me feel so much?
When did those stories stop being cold
And start to really touch?

Even kids' films catch me off guard these days
I see the writer's point of view
I guess I've lived enough now to understand
Whereas before I had no clue.

Lovely Garden

The backyard blooms in tangled weeds
The grass is left to grow
Every stem remembers us
And secrets only seasons know.

We wandered worn-out neighborhoods on foot
Through biting winter in the snow
When walking six feet side by side
Was the closest we could go.

When spring rain tapped on fogged-up panes
We built our forts from kitchen chairs
One day, we took them down
Unaware it was our last fort day there.

A couch once held by rope and prayers
Beneath the crooked trees
Cradled conversations shaped
By summer's tender breeze.

Fall evenings in our kitchen
Jars lined across the wall
Tomatoes, corn, zucchini
Aren't nearly as tasty
As the stories I recall.

The black minivan waited in every driveway
Its leather lining soft like a jacket I wore
I'd recognize that engine from miles away
A sound I can't ignore.

Through valleys in the fall, we chased the trees
Long drives that felt like leaving the world behind
Road trips stitched into memory like seams
A constant in a life I couldn't find.

Nostalgia grows in lovely ways
Where common eyes see none
The beauty is our mind's photograph
Each and every one.

The loveliest of gardens
Doesn't need the roses neat
It thrives where love has walked before
And made the weeds complete.

Loss Is a Friend

Loss is a friend, grief my companion
It's not a storm that passes
It's the weather I wake up to
It either drizzles behind my smile
Or soaks everything I do.

Grief is never gone. It's simply moved in
It lives in my chest, neighbor to my will
Some days it whispers, so I get close to hear
Only for it to then deafen me
Making me wish I had steered clear.

But I don't beg the skies to dissipate
I've accepted my new plus-one
We stroll through the hurricane
On solid ground until the clouds are gone.

My loss, my friend
We walk hand in hand
A solemn bond forged in long goodbyes.
Recovery I find
Isn't a place you arrive
It's rather a road with no destination
With mile markers of
"I got through today" despite hesitation.

Me and loss, we don't fight like we used to
We sit together now
Wait out the turbulence we've grown accustomed to.

Sitting with despair, I no longer demand
It vanish at my heart's command.
Now I know, it's not defeat
To let pain rest and take a seat.

SECTION TWO: ROUGH EDGES & GENTLE HANDS

Sometimes the hardest hands to hold are your own.

Loud Hearts, Quiet Voices

I speak in thunder, they answer in hush
I pour out my soul, they whisper: "Too much"
I'm not trying to drown them, I swear that I'm not
I just don't know how to half-feel a thought.

My heart kicks down doors, where theirs barely knock
I call it connection, they call it shock
I walk in with fire
Hoping for the warmth that they'll stay
But smoke seems to send the quiet away.

They ask for an inch, I give a mile
When someone tells me they care
I assume they'll stick around for a while.

The thing about those who love deeply
Is that their agony is great also
So when someone they cherish leaves
They always want to follow.

Please don't mistake my giving as desperate or weak
It's the language I was born to speak
It may come from lack, but it's honest and true
A love born of longing still knows what to do.

Quiet voices speak in careful tones
Afraid that too much might tear them in half
They say they feel things just as deep
But they bury the proof where no one can grasp.

I don't understand loving with a filter
How does one build a dam
As gushing emotions overflow and slam?

So if my noise scares off the quiet, I guess let them run
I can't change who my thunderous heart has become.

Why Share?

"Why put this work out there on display?
Why sing your songs if you're not getting paid?
Why share private pieces for strangers to read
If they're messy and rough and not poetry degree?"

Because I know how it feels to find yourself in a line
A moment you didn't expect
So if someone else is searching for that
I want to give them the same effect.

Besides, if greatness was needed before we began
No music would ever live past the voice of one man.

Mona Lisa was just a woman
Painted by a hand like any other
Likeness caught in simple paint
Became a gaze we yearn to discover.

Art doesn't ask for a flawless hand
Or excellence or logic
Only emotion
It asks if you understand.

To write is to give my experiences
A life of their own
So they don't have to
Dominate mine anymore.

And I don't need to shine to cope
I carry imperfect art with perfect hope
So I'll put it out even if it's not ideal
Maybe it will give someone else
Permission to feel.

Applause

When no one's around
What I make feels worthy of a stage
Applause erupts inside my mind
A crowd that I can gauge.

But if the quiet breaks
And real ears take my dream away
I'm scared they'd laugh at what I love
Turn my warmth into cliché.

Admiration feels counterfeit
I twist it, tear it down
Convinced they lied to spare my feelings
They're just good at hiding frowns.

What if my hands create a thing
The world calls dull or small
Was I fooling only me?
Was there no gift at all?

So do I leave it untouched
Where no one disagrees?
Protected by delusion
That belongs to only me?

Or do I risk the sting
Of knowing what I might not be able to bear:
That I'm no better
Than the silence filling empty air?

Applause could mean I’m brilliant
Or relief I'm finally done
They might just clap
To mask the fact that I’m the failing one.

And yet, without a soul to hear
I’ll never truly know
If all this noise inside my head
Is truly praise or just for show.

She Is Beauty, She Is Grace

She is beauty, she is grace
A whirlwind you can't suppress
Always a little late despite her efforts
Always in a wrinkled thrifted dress.

She lives to serve, craves to live
She's fighting every day
She's giving more than she has
Just trying to find her way.

She is beauty, she is grace
She is everything and more
She's too much and not enough
A locked and open door.

She's trying hard to keep up pace
Still somehow falls behind
She's wiser than her years suggest
But relief is hard to find.

The sweetest peach some ever meet
Too bright for simple eyes
The taste might haunt your thoughts
Or vanish like sunrise.

She is beauty, she is grace
Sometimes red, sometimes blue
Tangled. Not damaged. A work of art.
How it looks depends on you.

Imagine a Girl

(A love letter to me)

Imagine a girl
Who loves as fiercely as she lives
Infectiously magnetic
Standing by just to give.

She is many things to many people
Give or take, more or less
Who's to really say truth?
Who calls her wonder? Who calls her mess?
Well, here are some facts
So go ahead, make your guess.

She laughs at funerals
Sobs watching cartoons
Keeps phone notes for every little thing
Collects diner mugs, pinecones, and random spoons.

Tracks every detail
Of the people she loves
Forgetting them
Is what she's most scared of.

Believes all good things
Always fade too fast
That any dream of hers will never last.

Owns endless keepsakes
Of varying size and worth
Each one a portal to memories
She fears losing on Earth.

She'll laugh at anything
Especially if it shouldn't be funny
Her personal motto:
"Life is serious enough already."

Her greatest foe is her own mind
It will inevitably betray
Erasing anything and everything
She begs to stay.

Clinging to rusty anchors
She picked out on her own
Holding on for dear life
Regardless if they pull her down slow.

It doesn't take much to make her glow:
Shiny stickers, blowing bubbles just because
Finding little moments to smile
No matter what the day does.

She's lived ten lives
None of them safe
Each one a battle
She barely escaped
Little by little
She turns her life upside right
Giddy in the small things, hunting delight.

Imagine a girl who
Laughs at a sneeze
Finding the sound
Just silly and free.

She's made herself cry
With imaginary tales she'd spin
Entire worlds in her head
She'd happily live in.

Her Barbies wore capes
Her dice had their names
Little round people
In make-believe games.

Even now
When the contests are run
She's a sore winner deep down
Just needs to say she won.

Imagine a girl
Who studies love
Like it's a pop quiz
Always behind
Never sure what she missed
Scribbling answers
She thinks will be right
But love changes rules
In the middle of the night.

She craves to be remembered too
As someone she'd look back on and value
As the person she needed when she was small
Who would catch her if she happened to fall.

Imagine a girl
Who gifts devotion with ease
To everyone else
Yet struggles to show
That same love to herself.

The Mirror Doesn't Ask

The mirror doesn't ask me
What I'd choose if I could pick:
To see pure beauty looking back
Or someone gross who makes me sick.

I'm not asking this as metaphor
Although it sounds bizarre
Would you rather feel you're lovely
Or have others think you are?

To smell divinely to yourself
Perfection on the skin
While everyone else avoids you
Swearing something rots within.

Or trade it—let the world adore
The way you seem to shine
While every time you're left alone
The glass shows something vile.

They'd see someone stunning
Swear on their lives you smell
Like flowers in full bloom
While only you would gag alone
On rancid scents inside your room.

The mirror doesn't actually offer choice
It traps you either way
I'm so tired of caring
What it wants for me to say.

Love yourself, so they can call it pride
They'll tear you down with ease
Or hate yourself, so they say instead:
"You're beautiful! Please believe!"

Maybe it's a waste to ask
Which of these would scar me less
I'd only choose to never face the frame
That makes this awful mess.

We Are Not the Same

If I wear makeup, I'm trying too hard.
If she does, what creativity! She's so avant-garde.

If I order a salad, it's because I'm ashamed.
If she does, it's discipline. Beauty maintained.

I ask for an extra side dish, and they roll their eyes.
She eats the same? What a charming surprise.

Tight clothes on me? A walking offense.
On her, it's allure. It just makes sense.

I speak of self-love, so I must be trying to cope.
She says the same, her words glow with hope.

I'm "brave" for laughing loud, for speaking openly.
She's just confident—it's how she's meant to be.

They pair me with leftovers, with what's "left to take."
She dates whomever comes along
And it's romantic, not fake.
If I'm adored, they question his taste
If she settles, he's considered blessed by her grace.

She sweats, and you see shimmer, a glistened brow.
My sweat becomes shame. "Try harder now."

She talks passion, and they lean in close.
I do the same—“how sad,” they suppose.
She speaks her mind, they applaud.
I do the same, and they stare, maybe nod.

She compares herself to runway queens
While I compare myself to the space in between
Just hoping to pass, to still belong
Folding myself where I don’t fit in at all.

I’m handed beauty’s chosen mold
The girl I’m supposed to be
A version of myself I chase
But never quite achieve.

“She” is not a girl I watch and judge
She’s just my fantasy
The me I build in thought
Who lives more easily.

Although we share this skin
We are not the same
Maybe we just weren’t meant
To fit together in the frame.

DARE

How dare something as vital
To survival as self-image
Be dependent on something
As volatile as other people?
The scaffolds of my worth collapse
When others choose to be lethal.

I am too harsh to judge myself
They are even harsher than me
So how can I measure esteem
Count out what's what
When both are blind and cannot see?

How dare the things I deem
Necessary for my happiness
Be so bold as to be out of my control?
What tyranny, to starve my veins
Yet flood another's cup until it's full.

Here I am: rich in longing
But in loving: robbed and dull
I water roots that only break apart
Feeding gardens that will never
Make me whole.

How dare what I need for contentment
Reside in a stranger's view
When even my own eyes betray me
With lies I believed were true?

People innocently tell me to borrow their vision
They say it could set me free
Yet they are the first who shattered
The glass that defines me.

HOPE

(The day-to-day kind)

Hope. It makes contentment impossible
For it requires recognizing dissatisfaction
With where you are
It bestows you with visions of better
While breaking down any peace in the present hour.

Dreams built on what's next
Unravel what we know
Every glance at tomorrow
Is a theft of today's control.

Without the admission of deprivation
Hope would cease to exist
By giving it a name
Acceptance slips through the fist.

Hope feeds on hunger
To want is to whisper "not enough"
Satisfaction hides
And you're left calling its bluff.

It's a bargain, really
That empties while it claims to fill
Every little promise is only there to test your will.

It crowns you with futures
Stealing every present thing
It hands you tomorrow
While today takes wing.

I keep buying hope though
Even if it never pays
'Cause even a false tomorrow
Outshines my empty days.

Always Running

Always running
Never still
Can't slow down
Never reaching the top of the hill.

Perpetually behind
Skip every pit stop
At some point, it should get easier
But I still run 'til I drop.

Chasing both necessity
And the whims that pull at me too
Half-given effort at both
But I so badly want to follow through.

Must succeed each time
Must break through every wall
Must say I did my best
Must stand after I fall.

Slow down, face the mess
Or outrun every weight
Stop and meet myself?
I'd rather move before it's too late.

"Rest by choice," they say
Not when you hit the ground
Burnout won't announce
It arrives without a sound.

If I don't slow down
My body makes the call
At least then no one gets to say
I never tried at all.

Running feels like safety
Adrenaline numbs affliction
Priorities collide
The race is my addiction.

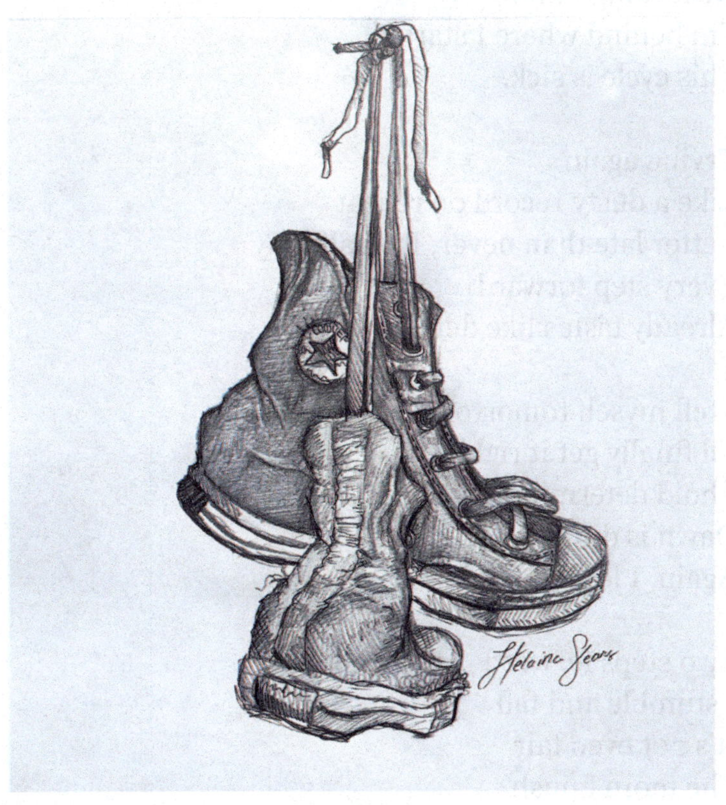

False Starts

I swear I'm gonna change
Say goodbye for good to my old ways
Wake up with a plan
Take control of my life
Own better days.

Morning quickly turns to noon
Effort fades quick
Next thing I know
I'm behind where I started
This cycle is sick.

Trying again
Like a dusty record on repeat
Better late than never, I usually say
Every step forward
Already tastes like defeat.

I tell myself tomorrow
I'll finally get it right
I hold determination at gunpoint
Dawn is dragging doubt behind it
Again, I lose the fight.

Two steps forward
I stumble and fall
It's not even fair
The more I push
The less I stand tall.

I can't even call it progress
Scraping my way
Every battle I win
Feels like a price
I can't afford to pay.

I guess false starts
Are just that, then
Disturbingly repetitive
But each one brings you closer
To progress again.

Pebbles

I was the girl mesmerized
By the glow across the sand and shore
I was the girl who kept believing
Every pebble held something more.

I carried them away
But all the glimmer vanished with the sea
Their beauty stayed behind
And left my eager hands empty.

My pockets full of treasures
Worthless only once I hold them near
Yet I cannot let them go
Even when their sparkle disappears.

Perhaps their glow was never real
Just something I chose to see
A brightness born of hope, not truth
But still it mattered much to me.

And if I drop them back
I know the next one calls my name
So why pretend I won't return
To play the very same old game?

How can it be deemed a loss, if it never became mine
Yet feel so useless once I keep it
Stripped of all its shine?

With people, as with pebbles, I hold tight to what I see
Believing in their shimmer even when it fades from
me.

Glimpse

When I look into my bedroom window from outside.
When someone else takes my car for a ride.
When I return from a long trip to the smell of home.
When I hear my own voice through a glitchy phone.
When my friends wear clothes I let them borrow.
When someone returns advice I gave as if it was their own.
When I see pictures taken of me when I thought I was alone.
When I read my own handwriting in journals I forgot I wrote.

Have you ever seen yourself without a mirror, like a clone?

Matter of Time

I'm already mentally preparing
When I sense good things getting too real
I'm confident they'll vanish
They usually do
It's for the best I don't let myself feel.

I try to lean in
But I can't help being on guard
Every time I've trusted
Enjoyed the moment
The goodbye hit way too hard.

I let someone close
Think this time will be different
But they eventually walk away
Leaving all my fears consistent.

Next thing I know
I'm back at square one
Swords drawn, ready to defend
Fighting off the hoard of doubts
That never seems to end.

It's really hard to love without holding back
When you expect the inevitable fall
To enjoy good feelings
To not catastrophize
To not grab bricks for that mental wall.

All good things are a matter of time
Gone before they fully arrive
A countdown ticking
To some assured unseen crime.

I'm physically near
But my mind is packing to leave
Counting every moment
Eyes on my watch
Getting ready to grieve.

I catch myself pulling back
Before I'm pushed away
The same pattern is all I know
Keeping my distance
Though all I want is to stay.

Things I Never Said Out Loud

I learned very young what words could do
One twist and the walls rearrange around you
Every question a trap
Every answer a reason to snap.

I was so scared of saying the wrong thing
Or hearing worse in return
So I shut my mouth
When I should've stood my ground
All my clever rebuttals came too late
Heard only by bedroom walls and shower sound.

I eventually got tired of cowardice, of holding back
So I tested the waters and dove right in
Now I don't run from speaking my mind
I let how I really feel pour out again.

Now I talk too much and too fast
I overshare to feel less small
Figure it out as I go
To trick myself into feeling heard at all.

If I don't say it, who ever will?
My forehead doesn't broadcast what I feel
I won't add to my regrets
Or to the cuts I keep concealed.

I talk like I'm digging free
Letting all my doubts be allowed
To make sense of and make up for
All the things I never said out loud.

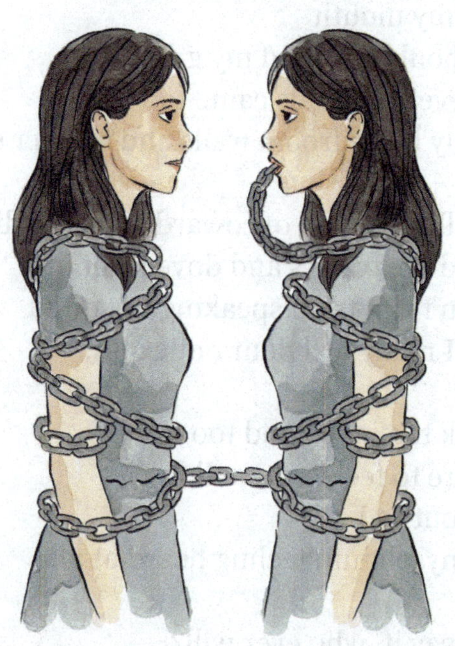

Finding My Pink

They say when pink feels safe
It's a sign of proper healing
When the shame and secret battles
Wave white flags and start receding.

I felt it first in little ways
With virtual pets I'd tend
Re-reading books from younger years
That made me fall in love with life again.

I drive with curlers in my hair
Pedicures in summer shine
I don't shop; I hunt
With no one 'round
To rush this joy of mine.

I laugh in aisles of floral prints
Pastel ribbons, beaded strings
The kind of things I once condemned
Now feel like small wings
Life is so much brighter
Enjoying all the little things.

I chase the shelves of childhood games
Without a hint of shame
Every choice that once felt strange
Now hums my younger name.

I sing out loud to pop-rock tunes
That once lit fires when I was ten
Songs my sixteen-year-old self
Swore she'd never like again.

Somewhere deep, that little girl
Is holding hands with who I am
Humming along in the outside world
A song we both now understand.

She can chase unguarded whims
Dancing barefoot on the lawn
Spinning freely through autumn winds
Where every heavy thought is gone.

Confidence Isn't Loud

Those who yell the loudest
Swearing they don't care at all
Are often climbing shaky steps
Afraid they're bound to fall.

Confidence walks softly
It won't beg to be believed
Its substance is not a fragile thing
That's granted or retrieved.

I wonder... is it simply that
New confidence feels strange?
A dazzling, rare experience
We're eager to exchange?

Or maybe we're just screaming
To be seen and understood
Impatient for the world to see
What we already could.

Stable self-assurance doesn't need a banner
Or to put others down to stake its ground
Nor does it tremble
If approval isn't passed around.

Real strength is to know yourself so fully
That no voice can drag you down
That is confidence
It doesn't make a sound.

Freedom

Contrast is the crevice
In which dimension likes to hide
The sum of opposites
Where only love resides.

Freedom is duality
That stretches our scope and view
Within our contradictions lies
The liberty to choose.

Some claim hypocrisy and
Contradiction are the same
I say:
Hypocrites act like what they're not
While contradiction carries two *truths.*
Both boiling hot.

Freedom dances at the edge
Of everything we know
It bends the path we think is set
And teaches us to grow.

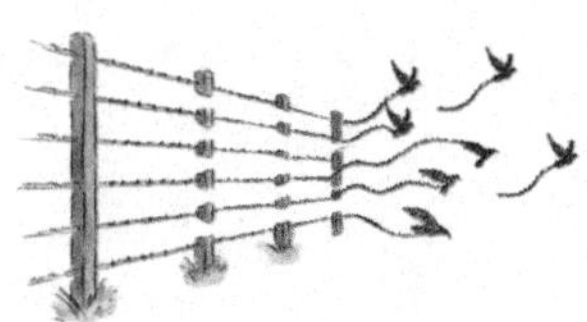

Balance

Ice cream by the fire
Car windows down, heat on blast
A perfect day = blazing sun
And frozen breeze that lasts.

Ice cubes in my soup
Fan in my face through winter nights
Sweaters worn in mid-July
Sand in my toes, jacket zipped tight.

Bookshelf alphabetized
Closet in disarray
Sad music lifts my spirits
Road trips chase away the gray.

Growing up with blizzards in April
Heat waves in October
You learn to bend with weather
Otherwise get crushed by its cover.

Chaos is my comfort
Dysfunction is my normal
My only routine is breaking them
My balance is in turmoil.

The Chase

For some, the chase is life
It is the purpose, the ultimate goal
But how can you measure success
By something only halfway possible to possess?

It must be miserable
To watch your dreams decay
Pep-talking yourself out of the same hole
Day after day.

Are they even living?
Always waiting for a future never seen
Thinking "something must be wrong with me."

I can only say I partly understand
Lack is not a stranger to me
He likes to come around and play
But I'd never invite him to stay.

No amount of friends or family can fill
The hole in their lives they chisel out
For their knight in shining armor
The damsel they call their own.

I could chase a hand to calm my crazy too
Or beg for love to sit next to me
I run instead toward my own quiet
I chase a different kind of serenity.

SECTION THREE: FIRST SNOW, BURNT TONGUE

Every last butterfly with your name on it
has finally flown away.

Not Yet

I long to be chosen
I hate that it matters this much
I say I don't need anyone
But I daydream to love songs
Like everyone else.

I relate to Jo March
I pride myself on standing alone
On guarding my peace like a fortress
No one undeserving can own.

I chase my ambitions freely
Find fulfillment in what I create
I tell myself I don't need unstable passion
Regret has never looked good on me anyway.

More times than I'll admit
I give in to the notion...
That someone worth admiration
Would choose me and crave my attention.

I imagine trading solitude for company
Independence for compromise
Privacy for vulnerability
Certainty for possibility.

But I've only ever been wanted
By those not worth wanting
Those that I could see myself with
Always end up being someone else's gift.

So I tell myself it's just not for me
Not in this lifetime
I'll find rest in my own rhythm
Create my own storyline
And a life without him.

Usually, it works
I don't feel absence like a wound
But then someone comes along
And I wonder if maybe, maybe soon.

Maybe he's the one the poems spoke of
The one who'll stay when others left
A stand-in for every daydream I folded away
Every "what if" I told myself to forget.

And just as quickly as he appears
I'm handed another "not yet"
Another "not this time"
And I'm left behind
Trying to keep what I want at a distance
Trying not to mind.

The Pot

They say a watched pot
Will never quite boil
So I keep myself busy
Pretend not to toil.

I sweep up the corners
Whistle while I wait
Try not to glance sideways
At everyone else's plate.

I clean dishes
Fold clothes
Do anything but stare
At the silence that grows.

I cheer for the couples
The glances, the rings
Then I fold up the sore
That comparison brings.

I keep my flame low
Set the pot on the heat
I stir things around
Keep moving my feet.

Some days I forget
That I'm even alone
Some nights I remember
And cry out to the unknown.

I tell myself: "Patience"
"Just give it more time"
"Your story is coming"
"You're still in your prime."

The hours keep passing
Nothing starts
No bubbles, no rising
No soft melting hearts.

Is the flame even on?
Did I miss the first sign?
Or am I stirring a pot
That won't ever be mine?

They say it'll happen
When you least expect
But how do you stop wanting
What you can't seem to forget?

So I keep on pretending
To care less every day
Though hope simmers low
In the back of my brain.

I tell myself one day
I'll long for this hour
The hush before rising
The stem without flower.

But I'm tired of lessons
Of growth, of delay
I'm tired of knowing
It's not yet my day.

I know it'll happen
I know that there's still time
I just wish it were easier
Living life 'til you're mine.

Just Friends

You don't like me.
You just like to talk to me.
You're not attracted.
I'm just easy to see.
You're not flirting.
We both crave attention.
I don't make you laugh.
That's just your own tension.

You don't like me.
I just make you feel tall.
You're not drawn to me.
I'm just easy to call.
You're not flirting.
I just care what you say.
I don't make you better.
I just don't look away.

You don't like me.
You just like the thrill.
You're not attracted.
I just sit still.
You're not flirting.
But I wish you had been.
I liked you.
But the minute I said it
We were always just friends.

He Loves Me Not

He loves me not, he loves me not
I won't dare forget it
I say it 'til it loses meaning
Then say it 'til I regret it.

It's just a glance, not something deep
A joke he made, don't overthink
A smile, a keepsake, a passing note
None of them signs. Just random ink.

He loves me not, he loves me not
I whisper when he laughs
I don't reread the way he spoke
Or second-guess the past.

I've hoped before
And hoped too loud
I've chased the wind
To be burned by smoke
I've built up meaning out of dust
And broke my own heart on jokes.

He loves me not, he loves me not
It's safer to believe
It hurts much less to walk away
Then wait for him to leave.

Then again, sometimes I'm wrong
Sometimes his stare lingers too long
Sometimes he's nervous, just like me
But I dismiss it. Danger is in the "maybe."

He loves me not, he loves me not
It's muscle memory now
I say it cold, I say it fast
If he likes me, it wouldn't last.

And when he means it, when he tries
I brush it off, roll tired eyes
I've trained myself to never see
That love could reach as far as me.

He loves me not, he loves me not
I'd bet my pride it's true
And still... a part of me hopes not
And still, a part of me
Hopes he does too.

NOPE
NOPE
NOPE
NOPE
NOPE
NOPE
NOPE
NOPE
NOPE
NOPE
NOPE
NOPE

I Have Known Love

I have known love, but love has not known me
I've reached for hands that would not reach for me
I've called its name through many sleepless nights
And only ever awoke to a world
Untouched by my cries.

I've given pieces of myself, none returned
I believe they're better gifted than kept and burned
I've built myself up many a wished-for design
While love passed by and wasn't mine.

I have known love, but love has not known me
I've held on where others chose to leave
I've stood in doorways that remained closed
Yet waited outside, completely exposed.

I know its presence but not its embrace
My pulse has known many hands
But my arms, though outstretched
Only reach barren lands.

Even if I'm permanently waiting
I don't budge, though doubts may come
For someday love may turn and see
The one who knew it faithfully.

Precipice

I'm tired of standing on the edge
Forever looking down
Dreaming of the leap I crave
Yet scared of crashing to the ground
Let's end the guessing game
Of what's hiding beneath the floor
Let me touch the fire once
And still come back for more.

No one chooses gravity; it pulls without a say
They call it falling only once your balance slips away
You never see the bottom
'Til the air is rushing through
Could be a bed of petals
Could be something harsh and new.

Some enjoy the plunge
It feels like flying through the starry night
While I just close my eyes
And brace against the fading light
This time, I dove headfirst
Knowing I'd pay the price real soon
I kissed the gravel with open arms
When gravity was you.

I guess I thought the excitement of descent
Would be worth getting shattered in the end
For you, I'd always jump again and again.

I'd take a temporary joy followed by pain
Over fear-induced regret any day
So for now, I'll drift between
The knowing and the guess
Betting on the fall itself to teach me nonetheless.

Someday, when I look back on all I've lived
The marks I can't undo
I'll see the proof of what I risked
When I believed in you.

Though the cut was mine to make
I'd choose it once again
For even in the breaking
Love was worth the way it ends.

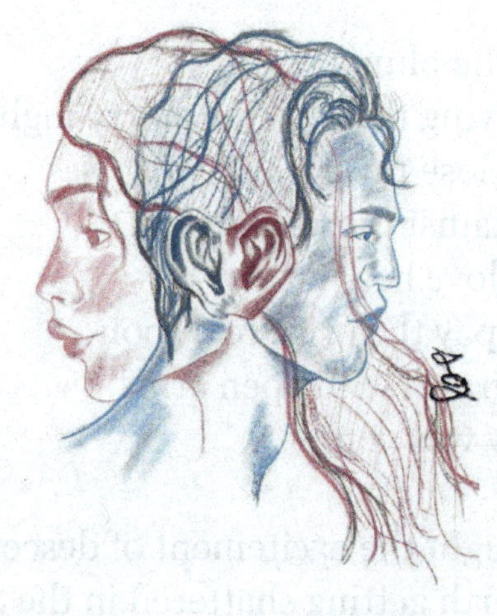

In the Fire

I chose to sit beside your flame
To burn with you, whatever it takes
Your heat, flaws, your stubborn spark
I welcomed all with a smile and didn't wince once.

This warmth would scorch others
Through and through
But I'd sleep on a bed of nails
And sweetly dream of you
I'd paint every inch of the sky a different shade of blue
If you simply looked me in the eyes and asked me to.

My friends nod and may voice concern
I hear them, I listen—I do.
But I stand firm. Not blind, but clear
For love is not what bows to fear.

Love knows well the art of stay
The stretch that knows no end
A restless wild bird
That never flies away.

I'd refuse your faults if worn by anybody else
For you, my limits bend and blur
Come what may
My grip remains secure.

Love knows tolerance by heart
It carries what it must
It stands unshaken in the fire
Where others turn to dust.

Worth Hurting For

I'd like to think you'd miss me
If I were gone
That something in your universe
Would always feel wrong.

I'd like to believe you'd struggle
Not knowing how or where I am
That you'd endlessly wonder
Dream of reaching me, knowing you can't.

I'd like to think
You'd have regrets if I left
That the void might
Steal something from your chest.

I'd like to know your life
Wouldn't be the same
If our paths never crossed
And you never saw me again.

I don't want to push you away
Not so deep down though
I just need to know
Would you miss me?
Would it be a fight not to call?

Is it possible to scar someone
With happiness instead of pain?
Let the wrinkles in your smile
Spell out my name.

TOO MUCH AND NOT ENOUGH

I'll never beg for your love
So I measure it this way
How much would it hurt
If I simply slipped away?

Will you crumble in my absence?
There's only one way to know
How quickly would you adapt?
Can I please be worth hurting for?

Maybe that's my little revenge
My silent counterblow
You get to leave a bruise
I never leave you at all.

I can't live with being some
Long-forgotten scene, fading out
I need to be engraved on your timeline
Etched into your story somehow.

I don't want you to be able
To look back on your life
Without seeing my face
Let me be a permanent sore spot
You'd never replace.

I don't want to torture you
Just soften your core
To be someone you long for
Worth hurting for.

Never Mine

They say if you love something
Set it free, wait in time
If it returns, it's truly yours
But you were never mine.

How am I supposed
To loosen what I never held
Pretend that I am fine
If what's slipping in between
My hands was never really mine?

You painted futures with your words
Promise in every breath
You spoke of wheelchairs
Broken bones, of sickness
Even death.

Now I dread to hear your name
Pronounced by anyone but you
Every secondhand account corrodes
The man I thought I knew.

You ruined stars and ruined songs
By teaching me their worth
You ruined all the things I love
By tying them to hurt.

I trace the bruise you left
Though pressing leaves me sore
The ache at least reminds me
Whom the love I gave was for.

You liked to call me your right hand
And here the truth shone clear:
I was always the first you'd trust
To see a plan or dream appear.

Strangers would glance and smile
Assuming what we were
A pair so stitched by ease
But too fragile to declare.

Now your ringtone chimes from someone else
The sound cuts sharp and deep
Here come the chest pains and a headache
From the rush of hope, then hollow grief.

You liked the myth of Icarus
Who reached but never won
Who soared too high, longed too much
And melted in the sun.

You knew that what we want the most
Will one day burn us through
And yet you fed the fire in me
Until I turned to ash for you.

One day, I'll see constellations
Without hearing the whisper of your breath
Without recalling cliffs or hours
Where joy felt close to death.

This wound will cease its bleeding
Though the bruise may never fade
No matter what I've lost or how broken I may feel
Someday I'll be okay.

Imaginary

I still wake up with things to say
That only you would get
I hear your voice in rooms
You've never been in yet.

It takes me days to feel okay again
When I have dreams of you
Like waking up in someone else's
Life I can't undo.

I see you in the empty seats
That strangers leave behind
You live in every second thought
That interrupts my mind.

I wonder if you fixed your sleep
Or still avoid the day
If we both find the night
More kind than what the sun might say.

I wonder, do I cross your mind?
Have you sealed that door?
Pretending I don't breathe at all
Is easier I'm sure.

I wish that I could do the same
Cut the thread you tied
I guess some connections
Learn to live in places we can't hide.

I talk to you in subtle ways
No one will overhear
As if you're still beside me
Like you never disappeared.

You'd make the only coffee I would drink
I'd fry the eggs just how you like
We swore the world could throw its worst
And we would be alright.

I wonder if you'd like this song
Or city, or café
If you'd laugh at things I'm thinking
That I'll never get to say.

I see you in the corners
Of the life I'm building now
Half-expecting you to ask:
"So, did you make it out?"

I pass by every car and think
That could've been your face
Then I feel ashamed for hoping
I never should have in the first place.

I play out every version
Where you stuck around and we were right
Not perfect, just more possible
Where we both could sleep at night.

First loves are never perfect, I guess
Just a little bit offbeat
Like shoes that don't quite fit
But you still don't want to leave.

Even when the air
Feels thick with everything I missed
I know you make it easy
By choosing to believe I don't exist.

Guess It Was Just Me

Guess it was just me
I answered his phone calls every day
I'm the problem; its my fault
For not keeping his affection at bay.

I am totally the one in the wrong here
Because I listened to all his secrets
I didn't push him away
Which is why I deserve to be abandoned this way.

Guess it was just me, then
I misread all the signs
Seven-hour phone calls, inside jokes left and right
Anyone after me better have been ready to fight.

But I should have just dismissed it
When he spoke of how happy we'd be
Just me and him, to be precise
When we got married
Hypothetically, you see.

Several people assumed
That we were an item already
What two friends need each other like that?
Without whom the whole world is unsteady?

So many think they know what went on here
So I'll take what remains
Those that really paid attention
They know I'm not to blame.

Sometimes I Miss the Misery

I miss the way I'd question
Every glance you threw my way
Some days it felt like love
Some like chance that didn't stay.

I miss the pleasant misery
Of whispers soft against my ear
You made me feel like
I was all you'd ever want near.

The signs I swore were special
Carved for me alone to take
But then you'd turn and tell me
All that hope was my mistake.

Just a friend who understood
The way your troubled mind would sink
Not the girl you pictured by your side
When the world began to shrink.

But better that cruel dance
Of almost-love and false delight
Than this abyss where we've buried
Even words that sparked a fight.

Sometimes I miss that misery
Potential disguised as promise
For at least I saw you then
While now neither cares to notice.

Sometimes when I catch a shadow
Shaped the way you stood
I swear I almost hold my breath
The way I always would.

Held My Breath Too Long

I held my breath for you
Until the air turned thin
Ashes of my lungs now left behind
Where hope and doubt begin.

I gave more than I had
Borrowed all I could
Just for resentment to fill the space
Where our relationship once stood.

I've held my breath so long
I don't know how not to
The anxiety is like a dance
Where hope and doubt hold hands.

Now every breath is shallow
Despite abundant air and sunshine
Impatient for a love
That might not come
Or ever die.

I guess all that time was wasted then
Spent chasing what wouldn't stay
Afraid to start again
Afraid to walk away.

My past now overtakes me
It reigns beyond its means
Measures people in the now
As victims of nostalgia: the Queen.

How can the hands of something never had
Choke until your eyes turn red?
When will visions of what could've been
Cease to keep me up in bed?

Someday history must forfeit its power
It shouldn't be this hard to trust
Someday a calm secure devotion
Will replace everything I lost.

But maybe I don't want it to
'Cause, then, that's the end of you.

But you've been gone for quite some time
And though I held my breath too long
I know I must move on.

Genie in the Bottle

Why do my eyes still widen first
When you walk into view?
If I am truly over this
Why do I still feel tied to you?

My pulse doesn't race like butterflies
But fight-or-flight instead
A familiar tightness in my chest I get
Each time your name is said.

Your hair's the same, your laugh unchanged
It echoes where you stand
I'd know your shape in any crowd
In any foreign land.

I knew you like the grass knows soil
Like clouds know open sky
Like suns know where horizons rest
Like birds know how to fly.

I knew you 'cause I can't know you
The knowing reached its end
As if you died, though you're alive
A stranger I call a friend.

Another holds the key you gave
Now she knows the man I knew
While I stand trying not to watch
Forgotten, out of view.

You once told me life felt bottled up
Your wishes trapped inside
I would swear you weren't as lost
As what you had implied.

I spent long nights consoling you
Convinced one day you'd see
But knowing I was right
Brought no escape or peace to me.

You say, "This is for the better."
I answered, "No.
You've run free from that bottle
While I'm sealed where you let go."

You got your longed-for ending
While I'm left all alone
Cork pressed tight
A genie left with no one else to hold.

Rearview

The road ahead is calling
When I glance behind, I see
Zombies of old decisions
Staring back, taunting me.

The warning on my rearview
Words I'm forced to face so clear:
“Objects in mirror are closer than they appear.”

Your silhouette teases me
In the frame beside my hand
Reviving parts of me I swore were lost
Like footprints in the sand.

Mirrors shrink miles to inches
Pulling you to me
A vision closer now
Then where you’re meant to really be.

Time says you’re far away
Yet every look betrays that lie
The past is leaning forward
While the present races by.

No matter how I press the gas
You’re never far behind
The tether of our history
Still weaves into my mind.

And though I drive to chase a life
That's begging to begin
The rearview makes it clear
You still live under the surface of my skin.

"Objects in mirror are closer than they appear"
That's why I can't help but flinch
When memories of you draw near.

The rearview isn't cruel
It merely tells the truth I missed:
That yesterday doesn't need to speak
To prove it stubbornly exists.

The seasons that stretch between us
Fold themselves into a crease
The memories I packed away
Come barging without cease.

Perhaps I miss you more
Because the mirror doesn't lie
You're not as far as the years
Or logic dare to quantify.

I Don't Want This

When you were gone
I could say that I was fine
It was easy to believe
Out of sight, out of mind.

I told myself I didn't love you
For a while, I really think I didn't
"I wouldn't have been happy anyway"
No compassion left to keep hidden.

Suddenly, you were here once more
And my brain clicked rewind
You're close enough to ruin me
Close enough to change my mind.

Suddenly, I remembered
The fight to resist
How hard it is to mean it when I say
I don't want this.

Suddenly, those words
Got stuck in my throat
They didn't come out smooth
They choked.

Hope and Pray

I hope you laugh
Without feeling insecure
With no weight in your chest
You feel forced to endure.

I hope happiness
Robs your storehouses of their grief
Leaving solace in its place
Like a long-lost belief.

I hope a safe stability
Chases away your nightmares
Replacing the screams
With soft morning prayers.

I hope realized dreams
Starve your sadness to death
'Til you barely remember
What broke you or left.

I hope your terrors
Don't follow you home
That peace floods the rooms
You once cried in alone.

I hope the music moves you to dance
Like the leaves are moved by the wind
Let the moment pull you off routine
With no need to hide or pretend.

I hope your quiet is calm, not lonely
I hope you find relief in places I never could
I hope love feels effortless, like I tried to be
Enduring in corners where mine never would.

I hope you never need
The kind of strength I had to learn
Or carry the remnants
Of bridges you burned.

I hope your days bloom bright
In ways I'll never see
That the light you chase
Is just a little too far from me.

May the life you build
Be richer than mine
I only request you spare me
The sight of your stars as they shine.

I sincerely hope every letter
You send me gets lost
Scattered like leaves
Unreached and uncrossed.

I hope and pray you get what you desire
Set your world completely on fire
I hope and pray your stories live far from me
So I don't have to watch or see.

I hope when you try to find me
You lose your map
Retrace every road
Then leave it at that.

Closet Space

I don't feel the need
To go through these things
I'd rather just burn all of our history
And the burden it brings.

I remember a time
When I'd smile at the sky
Thinking how grateful was I
To be yours.

Now, here we are
These empty pages of ours
And all the leftovers of that phase
Not even worth closet space.

I wish you'd come take your things
Yet it hardly matters anymore
Among this nostalgic clutter of broken promises
Are scraps of a life that will never be restored.

They used to mean so much to me
But now they all feel small
I wish I could ask if to you it's the same
Or are you stuck in it at all?

But I need to put things away
I've got sweaters, boots, and a vacuum too
We haven't spoken in years
My friends now don't even know you.

It's hard to believe
I'm saying goodbye to the last pieces of us
I'd rather toss them in the garbage heap
Along with the memories
I thought I'd always keep.

P.S. SECOND DEGREE

I waited for butterflies; this one brought hornets.

5.
(Hatred is kind.)

Hate is too kind a word
To describe how I feel about you.
Anger is too calm an emotion for what you are due.
Disgust is too fond a reaction to your sight.
Loathing flatters you. I'd rather it bite.
Rage would honor you more than you deserve.
Venom drips too sweet for what you've earned.
Spite feels playful. This is no game.
Even contempt is gentle next to your name.

I search for words sharper than words could be
Yet all of them falter, failing me.

22nd.
(The taking)

I said: “I’m tired.” You heard: “I can take more.”
You tore through my limits like breaking down a door
You lied with your voice, and you sweetened the sting
‘Til “want” meant “obey”
And your need was the King.

Every “don’t” you recast as a dare to persist
Each protest ignored, every warning dismissed
You didn’t ask. You just took what you craved
And called it my fault for not running away.

I froze in the moment, too trapped to resist
You carved out your desire and called it a gift
You dressed up your greed as a love I should seek
Turned silence to yes and my protests to weak.

You ate at my will like it kept you alive
Sick in the head with your need to deprive
You think you’re a lover, but you’re just a disease
And I was the host you refused to release.

You’ll say you were only in need
But need turns to greed when it learns how to feed
You smiled like you’d proven I’d wanted it too
But the truth is you took. Because taking is you.

SECTION FOUR: GLITTER SHOES & MUDDY STREETS

Blessings can always outweigh burdens.
You just have to learn how to see them.

Thicker Than Blood

This part is for those
Who taught me how to love
Gently. Fully. Fiercely.
With a strength that rises far above.

You've shown the world
You're proud to stand as my closest friends
Taught me that feeling deeply
Is nothing we must defend.

You've shown it's okay to stumble
To break, and to try again
That mistakes are the marks of learning
Not a final end.

That real love doesn't falter
Even when I'm hard to hold
It doesn't know limits of any kind
Neither young nor old.

To those who remind me to exhale
When life feels too heavy to bear
You steady my storms yet leave
My thunder floating in the air.

You teach my lungs to open wide
To trust that they'll expand
Guide me back to stable land
With your quiet (sometimes loud)
But always patient hand.

The way you trust me helps me
To trust the person I tried to hide
You inspire me to listen more
To give with open stride.

To hold a space that's judgment-free
To lead with calm, clear thought
Offer time and energy as gifts
That can't be bought.

You remind me good intentions
Aren't enough to make love whole
That what I give to others is the worth
I deserve to also hold.

You make my inner child feel safe
My grown-up self at ease
You've taught me that vulnerability
Is how real strength's released.

I've found passion in curiosity
Contentment among simplicity
Gratitude in all things
A constant rhythm flowing naturally.

I could never repay the many gifts
You have given me
When people say I'm brave or kind
I want them all to see.

I'll point to you and say "thank my friends"
The thicker-than-blood kind
For you are the ones who sharpen me
Who steady heart and mind.

Please Take It Personally
(Some gifts are just too big for one poem to contain.)

Anything can be funny
When your humor is broken
Broken people
Make the best jokes.

But you, you taught me how to laugh
With parts I used to hide
To giggle through the hurting
With you there by my side.

After all, we've earned the right to laugh like that
To turn bruises into punch lines
And trauma into a clever comeback.

I learned to love myself
By watching how you cared
You spoke so softly to that grown-up child
It's like the fear was never there.

You read stories to my anxiety
Until it curled up and fell asleep
You made safety feel simple
That kind of beauty runs endlessly and deep.

You're the reason I write snail mail
With glitter pens and real stamps
My future kids will all know your name
Because you're the reason I compliment strangers
And laugh mid-sentence without shame.

TOO MUCH AND NOT ENOUGH

You remind me not everything has to be
Life-altering to matter
Some of my favorite moments
Were found in the lighter chatter.

When something matters to me
You hold it like it's yours
That's how I learned
Love doesn't have to knock
It opens doors.

You taught me to raise my standards
Without lowering myself
To speak my name like a promise
Instead of pulling it apart
I'm excited for who I'm becoming
For once in my life, I'm not running.

Where my presence alone
Is enough to be seen
That's how I know I matter.
That's how I know what love means.

If you read these words
And think you haven't played a part
The title of this poem, I ask you
Read again with heart.

Like Night Needs Dark

You came along five years behind
Yet somehow you're the steadier mind
Though time says I should guide your way
You are the one who shields me day by day.

I need your joy the way trees need ground
Roots sinking deep where strength is found
The soil needs sun; the stream needs rain
I need you free from hurt and pain.

Like books need words to hold their spark
I need to see you safe, like night needs dark.

Like bridges need beams to stand and lean
Like fire needs air to keep its beam
Like athletes need constant protein
Like sails need wind to chase a dream.

I need you to be okay
Like oceans need tides to pull and sway
Like anchors need ships that won't drift away
I refuse to fight for you in vain.

If shadows ever steal your flame
I swear I'll burn instead and bear the blame
I'd tear down walls, I'd move the earth
Just to remind you of your worth.

Dear little brother who isn't so little:
I'll stand beside you, bend or break
Whatever loss, whatever stake.

For all I wish, for all I do
Is to see this world be kind to you.

Poetrice

You're not just in my poems, darling
You are the lines that reign
The ink that doesn't wash
The voice my rhymes obey.

You've heard all my darkest thoughts
Never stepped away
You stitched my edges up and taught my joy to stay.

I don't need complex lines to say the truth
I mean it plain
You're in my stories, in my jokes
Wired straight into my brain.

You give my heart a way to speak
Its chaos finds release
You've turned my thoughts to living art
That's why it's Poetrice.

Even when you moved away
I swear you're not that far
The breeze still calls your name to me
Like you never left my car.

You're my night-light in the dark
Steady when I'm scared
Because of you, I learned to face the unknown
Even unprepared.

I could no sooner count the reasons I love you
Than count the fireflies at twilight
Each flicker shines as evidence
Of how you make my world feel bright.

Jealous

You moved away and left me here
My love turned into spite
I'm jealous of the life you live
The people in your sight.

They get to see your smile every day
To hear your voice brand-new
While I am stuck replaying
All the moments I had with you.

I hate the thought of strangers
Now becoming what I was
Of someone else stepping in
Without a second pause.

Why did you come into my life
If you would just walk away?
Why show me what it's like to truly love
Then take that love and stray?

I miss you more with every day
That pulls you from my side
But I still pray your world is kind
And keeps your heart supplied.

I picture all the laughs you share
With people I don't know
I wish that I could be there too
To watch your new life grow.

They'll get to hear the stories
That I've enjoyed a thousand times
And see the way your eyes light up
When jokes and laughter chime.

I hate the thought of someone else
Becoming your "go-to"
The one you text at 3 a.m
The way I once had you.

I'm scared I'll just be someone
From a chapter you outgrew
A name you drop in passing
When old memories slip through.

I want to see you happy
Yet it cuts me like a knife
To know others now hold pieces
That once were all my life.

The Gazelle

Dorcas or Tabitha?
"Gazelle" is what her name meant
In my mind's eye
It's you a hundred percent.

She cared for the needy
Her kindness ran deep and wide
The ways you show love
Mirror hers, word and deed aligned.

Losing her brought heartbreak
That shook the earth below
So much that God declared:
'This is not yet a pain you have to know.'

The cries of those who knew her
Rose to heaven's gate
I'm certain the same for you
Our pleas would resonate.

A kind, self-sacrificing spirit
Used by God above
To lift and aid the weary
With steady hands of love.

The Gazelles within our ever-expanding family
Stand as pillars bright
Showing warmth, compassion, and joy
And you effortlessly embody that light.

Daughter, sister, wife, mother, or a caring, gentle aunt
I'm grateful for each seed of good
You've planted where hearts want.

My Home

Her hair is the shingles on the roof
That guard me from the rain
Her shoulder is the safest pillow
Where softest reassurance remains.

Her eyes, two kitchen windows wide
Where daylight warms my skin
Her smile is the open front door
That always invites me in.

Her laugh is the kettle on the stove
A delicious whistle that fills the air
Her feet are posts that hold the ground
Supporting me through every snare.

Her empathy is the key under the mat
Always there when I've lost my way
Her love feels like shoes by the door
Proof I'm meant to stay.

Her forgiveness is the spare room
She keeps ready for me
Her joy is the fire in the hearth
That outshines every star I see.

I don't need walls or wooden beams
Those that really know her will agree
My home was never built
She simply welcomed me.

Must Be Nice

We say *must be nice*
When someone else gets what we've been working for
It's not envy, but rather a gentle grin
A wink that says we see it and more.

Her: the lighthouse, steady and sure
Me: the ever-changing tide drifting toward her
We meet somewhere between calm and deep
Her order, my mess
A balance that somehow makes sense.

Her kindness runs on fumes
In such a way you'd never guess
She carries exhaustion like dust in light
Only visible when you look close, no less.

She puts in the effort others avoid
Cautiously, as if the world expects it from her
As if it forgot to say thank you
So it handed her another task to do.

When she laughs
The whole day forgives itself
Even the tired parts of me
Are restored to perfect health.

She's the reason I kept writing verse
The voice that said keep going
When I forgot why I started
She kept my stories flowing.

We joke that success skips our turn
But her friendship feels like winning
She's what I mean
When I say I'm not alone
She is my walking, talking home.

She deserves everything she desires
And I can't wait to watch it find her
Her existence alone warrants every good thing
That's why her nickname is my blessing.

Now it is nice
To have someone who gets it
Who meets me where I break
And entrusts me with her confessions.

Must be nice, I think
To know a soul like hers
To witness the comfort she brings
And watch how the world concurs.

Copy, Paste
(An ode to my mother)

You gave me shortcuts
Tiny codes I keep
I speak your syntax
In habits stored deep.

Traits you downloaded
To start my design
Some I leave as-is
Some I redefine.

You shaped my menu
With quirks I still load
Drafts we made slowly
Keep editing my code.

Your humor copied
Your patience pasted
Handed down files
Of all you created.

Your laugh, your ideas
Your way of repair
I find early versions of you
In margins everywhere.

Every lesson opens
Like a saved file
You built the basics
I format with style.

I catch my reactions
Just like you do
Sort thoughts the same way
With commentary too.

Same laugh at small things
Same stories retold
Same joy in colors
Same patterns we hold.

Your program hums
Behind everything I do
Updating each day
But still built from you.

Catdom

He is our Batcat, masked and bold
Revving like a lawn mower when he's consoled
A tiny vigilante with a grand routine
Acting like every sock obeys his regime.

Miss Ma'am, however; she prefers her throne
Claims my bed like it's her own
Drifting through rooms without a sound
Shakes off any trace of me as soon as I put her down
She tolerates my antics for a minute or two
Then trots off like she's got better things to do.

Two furry tyrants rule this house
One bold, both sly, running their domain
Both get scooped up into cuddle jail
Until I let them get away.

They always meet me at the door, tails high
Two shadows racing through the hall
Their purrs are my favorite lullaby.

Both curl at my feet when the day is done
A tiny fortress of fur and heat
Together, they make my whole world
Feel purr-fectly complete.

Never

I never want to have to remember you
Because you're always with me
I never want to talk about the good old days
Because we're too busy living them
I never want you in my past
I want you always in my present
I never want to miss you
Because we'll never be apart.

Testament

What I would give
To shelve you in the archive of my days
A volume kept within my reach
Forever on display.

Never borrowed out or cast aside
But waiting on my shelf
A story I return to
When I need reminders of myself.

But life is not a catalog where every book stays put
Its stories wander where they will
No matter how we look.

Some linger throughout our seasons
Some never hold their place
They vanish even when
We dust and alphabetize each day.

And here's the strangest thing
I've learned while keeping track
The books that look untouched
Are the ones that don't come back.

Their pages crisp, their spines unbent
Preserved in flawless grace
Not signs of treasured worth
But of a life no longer in my space.

The ones I love the deepest
Are the volumes worn and soft
Their covers creased from use
Their corners rubbed and scoffed.

Filled with notes from endless talks
Yet still feeling brand-new
Beauty not in how they looked
But in the fact they made it through.

Some bindings split from opening
From laughter pulled apart
Some signatures are fading
Where they pressed against my heart.

Is that evidence of love or the burden of it?
The untouched tomes remain sealed
Frozen in time's intent
While those I held closest leave proof
A lasting testament.

RACHEL MERRYN

Moonlight

You make others shine without a fight
Like the reflection of the sun
On the moon at night.

The moon doesn't produce its own luster
It merely mirrors the shimmer it's given
Don't ever doubt it, you are the reason
Those around you glisten.

We marvel at the sea
Its colors catch our eye
Forgetting it's only reflecting
The glory of the sky.

Take your sunlight wherever you go
The moon is not always in view
But your radiance continues to flow
Even when the sky conceals its blue.

Be careful, my dearest
Not to scorch or burn
You reach unexpected places
A glow that starts to heal and warm
Can leave behind harsh traces.

I'm Tired

When people ask me how I'm doing
I give the same reply
A shortcut version of the truth
I'm tired, that's why.

No one needs details
So I skip the full report
Of all the things that drain my spark
And leave me out of sorts.

But with my people
I don't have to explain
I can just let my body drop
And drift without restrain.

My best friend would visit
And knock out on my floor
That's how I knew she was my person
No one had done that before.

My brother doesn't say "I've missed you"
Not out loud, not straight
He just walks into my room and falls asleep
That's how he communicates.

My grandma couldn't chase us
Not when we ran all day
So she'd doze on the sofa
Just listening to us play.

My mom would pile us together
On her giant cushioned bed
We'd put something on the TV
And be out before the credits read.

When my dad spent his nights
In a place that wasn't home
We came every day to sit with him
So he didn't fall asleep alone.

Even my cats will curl close
And let me be their bed
Because love is that kind of trust
Where nothing needs to be said.

Sleep is its own language
That not everyone can read
It tells you you're protected
Without a single deed.

The Flicker Before the Flood

Before the words
Before the truth
There rests a line
Blinking like proof.

The insertion point
So it is called
You know the one
The blinking vertical line
On every computer screen
It allows the buttons on the keyboard to be seen.

The heartbeat of the page
A silent pulse, a waiting mark
Every story begins here
We all have a cursor inside
Some freeze before they ever start.

But the silent conductor with its baton
Cues the symphony regardless if it goes on.

That flickering spark
Guards what we dare to write
As if the tethers of our own mind
Are putting up a fight.

The tragedy was never
How your story ends
The real tragedy is never beginning.
It's silence that pretends.

Autumn Trees

I could live for days in awe of
Or among the autumn trees
Their colors heal my broken
Make life seem so open and free
I can feel my worries shrink to nothing
Under that refreshing canopy.

The trees—they talk to me
Wrapped in their vibrant coats
They tell me: "It's not your job
To keep the whole world afloat."

Until the day I saw a field of branches
Bright and spread
And for the first time
My problems felt heavier in my head.

I feel like a tree sometimes, so tired of holding on
I'd like to drop it all and let the cold come take me
'Til all my color's gone.

I've Always Loved the Cold

The cold always reminds me
Of love worth braving discomfort for.

This season often forces us
To linger in one space
It makes us sit across from each other
And finally speak face-to-face.

I love when it snows
Snowflakes muffle all the noise
They push us to discover
Unexpected joys.

I love the cold because
It gives birth to gratitude for warmth
It makes the small comforts grow
And settle softly in my arms.

Sure, it can be inconvenient
And may sometimes really bite
But I live for the moments
That turn the cold into delight.

Birdsong

It pierces my soul to hear birds sing
Knowing that they think night is day
Because the constant city glow
Distorts everything they know.

They chirp through a dark that isn't night
Confused by never ending light
Their instincts slowly stripped
They follow what they cannot fight
A dusk that's never quite right.

Aren't we much the same as they?
Simple creatures shaped along the way
By sounds and sights we're born amid
Reacting just as nature did?

We laugh at birds for whistling wrong
Then turn and judge each other all day long
For habits shaped by noise and glare
As if we chose the world out there.

No bird can turn the streetlamp low
No soul can change what they do not know
And both will sing, despite the eventual cost
Not knowing any better 'til their voices are lost.

Pinecones

They are flowers that never wilt
Shaped like hands, bent but built
A thousand forms, a thousand hues
Crafted by their Creator's muse.

Some see a whisper of God's loving heart
Delicate, a world apart
Others call them tree's discarded waste
Like tree poop, tossed aside with haste.

Some find beauty in the smallest things
A gift beneath the pine tree's wings
While others walk with hurried eyes
Blind to what beneath them lies.

In each curve, in every scale
A testament to how we're frail
For we, though made of dust and clay
Were meant to live beyond this day.

Pinecones, too, declare the plan
Seed bearers made by God's own hand
They fall but rise again; they thrive
A promise that life can survive.

For trees live long, their roots run deep
While we, through time, are forced to sleep
Yet these cones, like seeds, they fall
God's work endures, and gives life to all.

Their spiral shapes, their perfect grace
Remind us of a future place
Where we, like trees, will stand and grow
A life eternal just as we know.

What Is a Song?

A song is the only *universal language*
Made for feelings deep and unexplained
A *voice* that murmurs secrets
Speech has never really named.

It is the *bridge* across the void
Where words cannot dare to creep
Carrying shared emotions across the chasm
Syncing heartbeats.

A song is *time's own vessel*
Without a speck of fear in sight
A *capsule of an instant*
Bathed in memory's softest light.

It's *the twinkle in your eyes*
When someone else shares your choice
Singing side by side
It's *the smile in your voice.*

A glimpse into the infinite
A space for thoughts to speak without a tongue
The *melody of living*
This is what defines a song.

Music itself is the *amp of life*
That tells the story of who we are
My *soul's translation*
Without judgement, pure communication.

RED

The color of contradiction
Its duality mirrors the paradox we face
Speaking in equal parts of love and rage
That restless hue refuses to stay in one place.

A shade that honors even battles lost
While also long-held wishes finally claimed
We wear both sorrow and smile sincerely
Two truths that never needed to be tamed.

This primary color provides a primary reminder:
That grief and joy can share the same home
That contradiction isn't chaos, but color
And one truth doesn't have to erase another.

When we accept our emotions can coexist
We give them room to breathe instead of flee
To pass through without wreckage
And depart when they're ready.

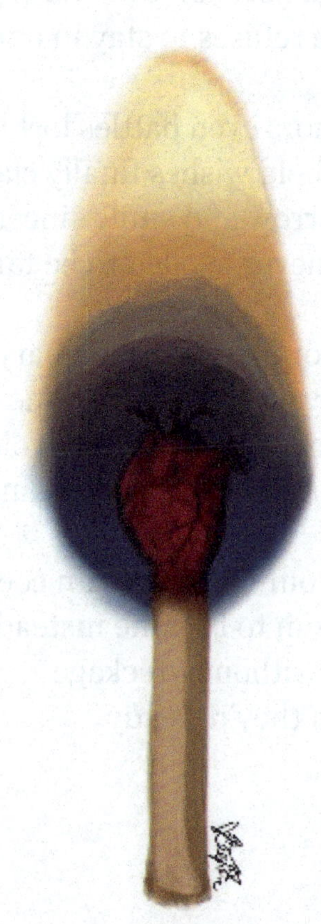

ACKNOWLEDGEMENTS

This collection is stitched together not only from my own words but from the presence of many others.

To those whose lives touched mine so deeply that they appear between these pages: You may never know the imprint you left behind.

To my mom: Thank you for setting the groundwork for me in more ways than I can count. Your creativity has fueled my own for as long as I can remember. So much of my courage to share these words comes from you.

And to my fantastic editor, Emily Reed at Peony and Prose Editorial: an extra note of gratitude for your detailed eye and constant support. I couldn't have done it without you.

AUTHOR BIO

Rachel Merryn is a bilingual author whose Greek and Scots Irish heritage shapes her love of words and wisdom. Beyond the page, she's a traveler, musician, and collector of life's small wonders. Always chasing stories hidden in ordinary moments.

Having worked countless diverse jobs, her most beloved role has been her current one at the library, where the hum of stories provides the perfect backdrop for her own writing.

A lifelong reader, she counts Rick Riordan, Jane Austen, Agatha Christie, Celia Martínez, Josie Balka, Corrine Dalton, and IreAnne Chambers among her many favorite authors.

Her pen name, Merryn, comes from Celtic origins and means "sea born." The name honors her Irish heritage while also reflecting the Mediterranean spirit of her Greek roots—bringing two worlds together in a single identity for her writing. "Merryn" is her tribute to the sea, to fluidity, and to the endless depths of feeling.

Greek Poem Translation of **Μανάρι**

Your Little One

When I was younger, I kept asking to leave alone
I thought life was waiting for me in the next town
I counted days, counted years
Waiting for the road to open
So I could say, "I grew up," without any trace of fear.

And yet, my father, now that time has passed
I see I was running from everything that was mine
No matter how firmly I stood on the legs I begged for
I turned back inside myself to the one I loved
Back to you.

And when you left, my father, your voice disappeared
And the music I loved slowly withered too
I want to go back, to hold on to that child again
Your little one
Who danced and laughed straight from her soul.

Made in United States
Orlando, FL
10 March 2026